150 Best Loft Ideas

150 Best Loft Ideas

Edited by Bridget Vranckx

COLLINS DESIGN

An Imprint of HarperCollins *Publishers*

150 BEST LOFT IDEAS

Copyright © 2007 by COLLINS DESIGN and LOFT Publications

HarperCollins books may be purchased for educational, business, or sales promotional use.
For information, please write: Special Markets Department, HarperCollins*Publishers*,
10 East 53rd Street, New York, NY 10022.

First published in 2007 by:
Collins Design,
An Imprint of HarperCollins*Publishers*
10 East 53rd Street
New York, NY 10022
Tel.: (212) 207-7000
Fax: (212) 207-7654
collinsdesign@harpercollins.com
www.harpercollins.com

Distributed throughout the world by:
HarperCollins*Publishers*
10 East 53rd Street
New York, NY 10022
Fax: (212) 207-7654

Executive editor:
Paco Asensio

Editorial coordination:
Bridget Vranckx

Art director:
Mireia Casanovas Soley

Graphic design and layout:
Anabel Naranjo

Cover design:
Claudia Martinez Alonso

Library of Congress Control Number: 2007935530

ISBN: 978-0-06-134827-3

Printed in:
China

D.L.: B-52.114-07

Second Printing, 2008

Contents

Introduction

Lofts have come a long way since they first appeared in 1950s Manhattan. Originally, abandoned warehouses and factories were colonized by artists who converted the enormous spaces into affordable homes for living and working. Nowadays, these lofts are among the most expensive properties in the city and are more likely to be inhabited by young entrepreneurs, graphic designers, and art collectors. Latter-day lofts, however, have also inspired a new way of living. With the increasing density of many metropolises and the reduced dimensions of residencies, lofts and their open often sprawling spaces are sought after these days. Those lucky enough to still find neglected or abandoned industrial spaces are transforming them into modern lofts in a range of different styles. Others living in more conventional homes are knocking down unnecessary walls to create airy, light-filled spaces, thus turning otherwise cramped living quarters into spacious open-plan layouts.

No longer the preserve of bohemians, the decoration of lofts has passed through myriad fashions, ranging from eclectic to minimalist and practical. As you'll see from the projects shown in this book, these days, anything is acceptable. Organized into five sections, the book opens with open plan lofts arranged on one level. The next chapter looks at the use of levels and partitions to make the most of a space's available volumes, followed by the introduction of custom-built objects and the use of color to identify different areas of the home. There are numerous ways of maximizing space and light, key features of contemporary living: Turn to the chapter on "Transparency" for some ingenious solutions and to the last chapter for a selection of unusual conversions. The 150 ideas throughout the book should help you make clever, efficient use of your space and organize it to suit your needs.

One Level

Nychay Loft

Architect: J. Tanney,
R. Luntz/Resolution:
4 Architecture
Location: New York, NY, U.S.A.
Date of construction: 2004
Photography: Floto + Warner

This home of a single young professional is located in a new loft building in the historic neighborhood of SoHo in downtown New York City. The design addresses the classic duality of an open loft versus partitioned intimacy reflected in the contrast between the sophistication of a contemporary high-end residential project and the characteristics of a structure that began as an industrial building.

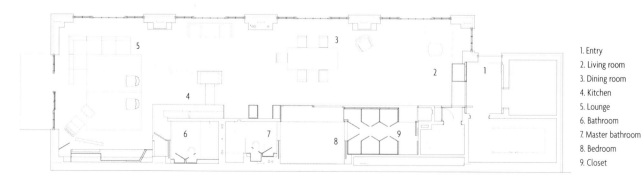

1. Entry
2. Living room
3. Dining room
4. Kitchen
5. Lounge
6. Bathroom
7. Master bathroom
8. Bedroom
9. Closet

Floor plan

Each space in the continuous living area is defined by different materials: a rosewood table in the dining room, a teak island in the kitchen, and a wenge wall in the living room.

A dense, complex box containing the kitchen and secondary spaces is placed on one side of the loft, which doesn't interrupt the continuity of the 66-foot-long living room.

3

The bathrooms, bedroom, and dressing room are modules built along the side of the loft and can be closed off with sliding and translucent partitions.

Dobinsky Loft

Located in Montifuri, an industrial area of downtown Tel Aviv, this approximately 1,076-square-foot loft was designed by the owner himself. The space is used for both living and working and is arranged as an art gallery so the artist can display his work like a permanent exhibition. The artwork and exhibition panels serve as simple dividing walls between the day and night areas.

Architect: Eyal Dobinsky
Location: Tel Aviv, Israel
Date of construction: 2006
Photography: Yael Pincus

4

The artist-owner's work hangs on exhibition panels that also function as dividing panels and "blinds" in a loft that is at once home, studio, and gallery.

1. Living area
2. Sleeping area
3. Bathroom
4. Dining area
5. Kitchen

Floor plan

Industrial Evolution

An old factory on ground-floor space in eastern Johannesburg, South Africa, was converted into a creative open-plan living space. Surrounded by large industrial buildings, this 98-by-59 foot space holds a generous residence, with two bedrooms and a bathroom on one end and a living room and office on the other, eastern, end.

Architect: Ron Prentice
Location: Johannesburg, South Africa
Date of construction: 2003
Photography: David Ross/Inside

Sun streams in through large industrial windows, which fill the north-facing facade. Brick, plaster, and rough black floors dominate the interior design.

6

Two bedrooms and
a bathroom are situated
at the western end of this
converted factory building.

Bachelor Pad

Architect: *unknown*
Location: Brussels, Belgium
Date of construction: 2001
Photography: Vincent T'Sas/
Inside

Modern furnishings and contemporary materials have been combined with raw industrial elements to create the perfect bachelor pad in the heart of Belgium. No luxuries or modern amenities have been overlooked to create the perfect atmosphere: a pool table, a theater-size television screen, and a generous kitchen. The feeling of spaciousness is maintained thanks to the open-plan layout.

Modern materials, such as the stainless steel used in the kitchen, live in harmony with exposed-brick walls and industrial elements like open duct work to create a contemporary loft.

A futuristic-style bed
and bath sit happily
beneath a vaulted,
exposed-brick ceiling.

Alon Kastiel's Loft

Architect: Kastiel Design
and Furniture
Location: Tel Aviv, Israel
Date of construction: 2006
Photography: Yael Pincus

This 3,229-square-foot loft is located in an industrial area of downtown Tel Aviv and was designed by the party-loving owner himself, who chose to maintain the feeling of openness in this loft. The living spaces are arranged in an open-plan layout and the more private areas can be separated by white curtains, which also lighten the palette of grays and blacks throughout.

Floor plan

1. Living area
2. Kitchen
3. Office
4. Bedroom
5. Bathroom
6. WC

White walls and curtains help give the space a feeling of openness, while an ample mirror in the bathroom connects this private room with the rest of the loft (see following pages).

A palette of dark colors combined with lighter tones and white create an elegant urban loft.

Well-placed pieces of antique furniture lend a touch of solidity to this huge industrial space, which is flooded with natural light.

Antwerp Loft

Architect: Werner van
Dermeersch, Carla van Mileghem
Location: Antwerp, Belgium
Date of construction: 2000
Photography: Bertrand
Limbour/Inside

An oblong industrial space is turned into a contemporary urban loft with a minimum of structural changes. The private space is separated from the main living space by a simple freestanding wall painted a bright blue. At the same time, the two areas are connected by a low cabinet that runs the length of the loft.

Polished concrete floors
and a metal-colored cabinet
running along the length of
the loft visually unite the
private and public spaces,
divided only by a
freestanding blue wall.

A smooth wall of built-in wooden kitchen cabinets houses all the kitchen utensils and appliances and makes this area stand out from the rest of the loft.

A colored wall serves
as a space divider as well as
a wall for the walk-in closet
in the sleeping area.

The Black Apartment

When Cindy Gallop, voted New York's advertising woman of the year in 2003, commissioned the design of her apartment, she had one overriding request: "When night falls, I want to feel like I'm in a bar in Shanghai." The designers came back with a bold vision which they expressed as an entirely black apartment. Mixed with plenty of display space for Cindy's art and objects, this 3,500-square-foot space is a fabulous home like no other.

Architect: The Apartment Creative Agency
Location: New York, NY, U.S.A.
Date of construction: 2005
Photography: Michael Weber

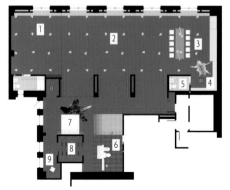

15

Instead of dividing walls, the space has a network of soundproof and sheer black curtains which give it an expansive, expensive, and expandable feel.

1. Library
2. Living room
3. Dining area
4. Kitchen
5. WC
6. Bathroom
7. Bedroom
8. Closet
9. Make-up room

Floor plan

16

The owner's impressive and eclectic collection of furniture, artwork, books, and designer stilettos stand out against black walls and curtains.

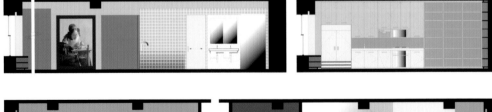

Sections

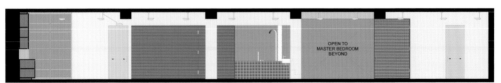

OPEN TO
MASTER BEDROOM
BEYOND

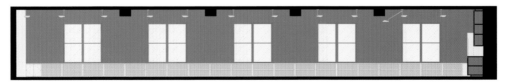

Sections

The owner's personality is clearly expressed in her home: a 250-pair shoe display, a bathtub on a platform, and a library kitchen are just a few examples.

INGREDIENTES:
- QUESO BRIE
- ROQUEFORT
- PARMESANO

Recycled Factory

Architect: Mercedes Cristiani
Location: Buenos Aires, Argentina
Date of construction: 2003
Photography: Juan Hitters/
Sur Press Agencia

Originally a toy factory, this home in the Argentine capital had morphed into a mechanic's garage for trucks and old cars when the architect first laid eyes on the space. Together with her husband, she wanted a different place to live and so decided to transform this place. Her mission: to create a unique family home with plenty of space for the children to interact and run around.

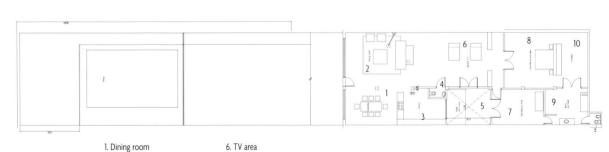

1. Dining room	6. TV area
2. Living room	7. Children's bedroom
3. Kitchen	8. Master bedroom
4. WC	9. Bathroom
5. Open-air patio	10. Dressing room

Floor plan

A large multifunctional loft-style space, illuminated by natural light integrates a living room, a TV-viewing area, a dining room, a kitchen, a children's bedroom, and an expansive master suite.

Changing-room-style showers in the bathroom work well in a high-ceilinged space. The intense green color of the door breaks up the smooth cement of the walls and floor.

Beach Street Loft

Architect: Dennis Wedlick
Architect
Location: New York, NY, U.S.A.
Date of construction: 2005
Photography: Elliott Kaufman

This former warehouse was turned into a warm residential environment for a growing family, using soft light in both its natural and artificial form. Louvered grills are used to modulate the light, a safer strategy for children than frosted glass; they add a layer of refined texture to help tame the existing rustic structure.

The long narrow space is controlled with multiple furniture arrangements. In the living room, a tête-à-tête divides the space.

Floor plan

1. Master bedroom
2. Master bathroom
3. Master closet
4. Bathroom
5. Pantry
6. Kitchen
7. Entry closet
8. Bedroom
9. Hall
10. Laundry room
11. Family room
12. Living room

Triangle Loft

Shaped like a triangle, the building at 675 Hudson Street is approximately 200 years old and was mainly used for manufacturing. Shadi & Company moved here in the mid-1990s and transformed the space into an architecture-design atelier, a fabrication shop, and a home for the architect, Shadi Shahrokhi. The space changes identity constantly: An office by day, it can easily accommodate by night a dinner party with live jazz for 50 people or become a dance party venue with a DJ for 200.

Architect: Shadi Shahrokhi
Location: New York, NY, U.S.A.
Date of construction: 2000-ongoing
Photography: Andrea Morini

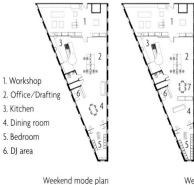

1. Workshop
2. Office/Drafting
3. Kitchen
4. Dining room
5. Bedroom
6. DJ area

Weekend mode plan

1. Workshop
2. Office/Drafting
3. Kitchen
4. Casual meeting
living room
5. Private meeting
listening room
6. DJ area
7. Meeting/Conference

Weekday mode plan

On the weekends, Shadi's living area spills over into the office area. The space is easily transformed again to accommodate the work space and all kinds of events.

Loft Bosco Sodi

The home of a former 3,229-square-foot printing works in the center of Barcelona was transformed into a 3,767-square-foot loft for a family of six, with five bedrooms, four bathrooms, sauna, laundry and ironing room, kitchen, bar, and dining/living room. The architects decided to maintain several elements of the original structure: Among other things, the roof was renovated, and the original trusses—previously hidden by false ceilings—and the brick walls were exposed.

Architect: Borja Carreras,
Dora Castellà
Location: Barcelona, Spain
Date of construction: 2005
Photography: Jordi Sarrà

1. Living area
2. Dining area
3. Office/Library
4. Interior garden
5. WC
6. Bathroom
7. Kitchen
8. Domestic's bedroom
9. Laundry room and pantry
10. Patio
11. Children's area
12. Children's bedroom
13. Office/Guest bedroom

Ground floor

The floors are covered with a layer of polished concrete, which recalls the place's industrial past and contrasts with the exposed brick walls.

23

The former freight elevator
was removed to make way
for an interior patio,
right, filled with natural light,
situated next to the entrance
to the loft and opposite
the kitchen, above.

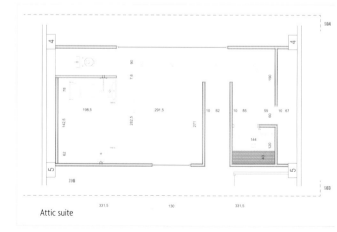

Attic suite

24

Skylights were cut out of
the renovated roof,
and two mezzanines on
metal superstructures above
the main floor were built
to house two of the
five bedrooms.

Objects
and
Partitions

Q Loft

Architect: J. Tanney,
R. Luntz/Resolution:
4 Architecture
Location: New York, NY, U.S.A.
Date of construction: 2004
Photography: Floto + Warner

rmer industrial building in New York's Chelsea neighborhood,
 loft for Joe Quesada and family occupies an entire floor and has
un the length of the space and dynamic urban views on three sides.
otprint is extremely large, the private zones abut three outer walls,
eaving public zones stitch them together.

A number of acrylic, internally lit, shelves are built into the back of the theater wall to accommodate the owner's large collection of comic artifacts.

Floor plan

1. Living room
2. Kitchen
3. Studio
4. Powder room
5. Utility room
6. Storage room
7. Bathroom
8. Bedroom
9. Playroom
10. Guest bedroom

11. Guest bathroom
12. Entry
13. Theater

14. Hall
15. Music area
16. Dining area

17. Master bedroom
18. Master closet
19. Master bathroom

The guest bedroom, child's room, and playroom all have interior clerestory windows to let in natural light.

26

The kitchen and living areas are divided and at the same time connected thanks to a freestanding island.

27

A semiprivate home theater and artist's studio sit between the private zones. The theater may be turned into a public space by opening the large sliding glass doors.

Fashion District Loft

This 1920s industrial space in New York City's Fashion District inspired the architects to enter into "a dialogue" with its high ceilings, visible structural elements and plumbing, and polished concrete floors. The major challenge and consideration in the design of this 1,500-square-foot loft was to maximize natural light. Thus, a sense of open, flowing spaces was created by means of tall, elegant sliding doors; translucent panels and architecture like the kitchen island that morphs into art.

Architect: Guardia Architects
Location: New York, NY, U.S.A.
Date of construction: 2005
Photography: Bradley Jones

1. Living room
2. Dining room
3. Kitchen
4. Pantry
5. Master bedroom
6. Closet
7. Master bathroom
8. Bedroom
9. Bathroom

Floor plan

The kitchen island, a central architectural element, is an origami-like sculptural form that seems to fold and unfold onto itself.

Loft Dassel

The architects of this loft, situated in the maritime quarter of Molenbeek, Belgium, have created a contemporary urban family home. The interior design has been carefully planned to the smallest details, all the while maintaining functionality and a pleasing aesthetic. The private areas leading from the main living space can be closed off, thanks to sliding doors with translucent panels, which provide privacy without sacrificing airiness.

Architect: **Laurence Sonck**
Location: **Brussels, Belgium**
Date of construction: **2005**
Photography: **Laurent Brandajs**

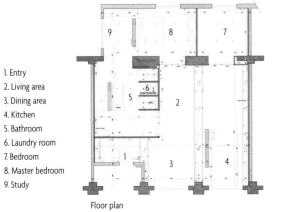

1. Entry
2. Living area
3. Dining area
4. Kitchen
5. Bathroom
6. Laundry room
7. Bedroom
8. Master bedroom
9. Study

Floor plan

A low custom-built wall separates the kitchen from the dining room; a pass-through allows interaction between the two spaces.

All the cupboards, shelves, and sliding doors are perfectly integrated into the overall design of the home.

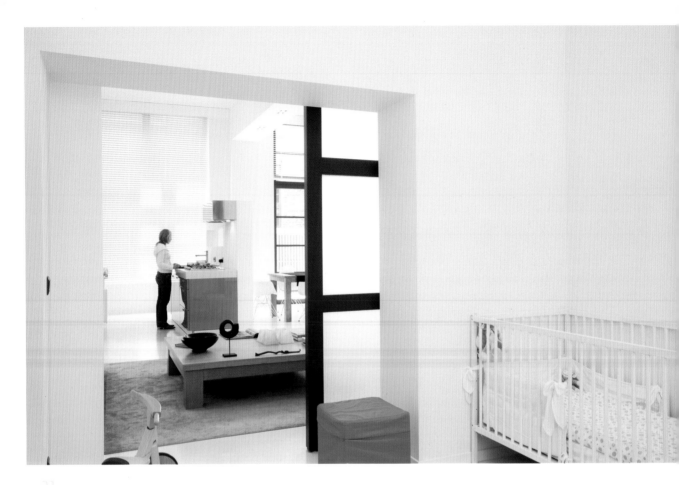

Every last inch of this home,
down to the careful lighting,
has been considered.
Spotlights have been
installed in the bed's
headboard and the
kitchen-dining partition.

32

Built-in cupboards blend
into the white walls
and are ideal for storing
the children's toys.

Loft in Buenos Aires

This huge loft located in the typical Buenos Aires neighborhood of Barracas used to be the garage of Bonanno, a company that built race cars. Behind the large front door lies a space of unusual dimensions—164 feet long and 23 feet high—where a father and his son have made their home and artist's studio.

Architect: Julio and Luciano Pérez Sanz
Location: Buenos Aires, Argentina
Date of construction: 2003
Photography: Virginia del Giudice

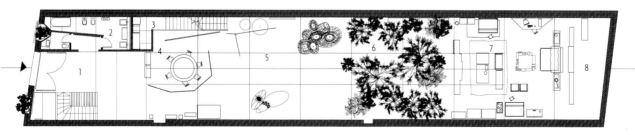

Floor plan

1. Entrance hall
2. Bathroom
3. Kitchen
4. Dining room
5. Multi-use space
6. Garden
7. Studio
8. Storage room

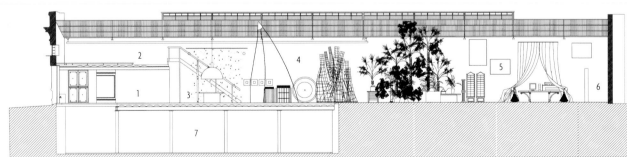

Section

1. Entrance hall
2. Bedroom
3. Kitchen
4. Multi-use space
5. Studio
6. Storage room
7. Workshop

Creating a beautiful, wild indoor garden in the middle of the long loft is an original way of dividing it into two distinct zones.

Decor inspired by the pomp
of the courts during the
time of the Catholic Kings
gives this loft a period look
with ethnic touches.

Art Collector's Loft

An art collector and yoga instructor wanted to gut a full floor of a former manufacturing building in midtown Manhattan and transform it into her working and living space. Thus, the architects had to accommodate a number of different uses and activities with 4,000-square-feet. The challenge of this open plan with interconnected spaces was to maintain a sense of openness and continuity without losing intimacy or privacy, as well as to adequately display the client's collection of art.

Architect: **Steve E. Blatz**
Location: **New York, NY, U.S.A.**
Date of construction: **2002**
Photography: **Sur Press Agencia**

Freestanding wood walls in
ash is one of the main
features in the design.
These tall structures,
which connect four
separate areas are clad
in horizontal ash strips.

Floor plan

1. Elevator
2. Entry
3. Kitchen
4. Yoga room
5. Living room
6. Studio
7. Guest bedroom/TV room
8. Freight elevator
9. Loading
10. Yoga storage
11. Art storage
12. Gallery
13. Laundry room
14. Office
15. Bathroom
16. Meditation platform
17. Dressing room
18. Bedroom
19. Terrace

Every room contains
a space for art.
The meditation platform is
an example of how the
architects transformed
the furniture into an
architectonic element.

Loft CL

Two-thirds of the loft carved out of this former industrial building has been left clear to create one large living space. The remaining third has been squeezed into a functional layout hidden behind a long wood-frame wall covered with metal cladding. A completely different kind of intimacy is found when someone opens one of the barnlike doors to find a raw space resembling an attic accommodates the bedroom, dressing room, and bathroom.

Architect: Jan Demuynck
Architecten
Location: Brussels, Belgium
Date of construction: 2005
Photography: Laurent Brandajs

The metal cladding, which covers the long wood-frame wall dividing the loft space, complements the original high ceilings, and exposed steel beams and brick walls.

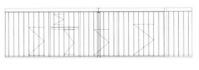

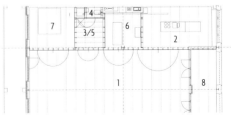

1. Living area
2. Kitchen
3. Storage room
4. WC
5. Duplex
6. Bathroom
7. Bedroom
8. Terrace

Floor plan

38

A series of doors
have been cut out of
the metal cladding
on the dividing wall.

39

Stepping through the barn-like doors, one enters a totally different atmosphere: a seemingly unfinished atticlike space for sleeping, dressing, and washing.

Ply Loft

In response to the New York predicament of too many functions in too little room, the architects of this 1,000-square-foot loft in New York's Tribeca neighborhood came up with an original solution. They created a sinuous surface of bendable plywood that weaves together existing columns and unifies various spaces. A wall of sliding screens helps control the intense daylight entering south-facing windows and allows the artist clients to project their video work out to the street.

Architect: nARCHITECTS
Location: New York, NY, U.S.A.
Date of construction: 2005
Photography: Frank Oudeman

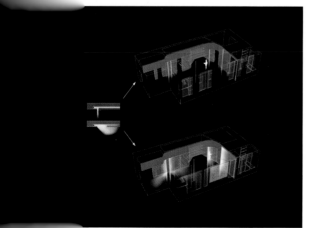

Flush sliding doors function as dimmers for concealed light fixtures in the door jambs: Opening and closing the doors modulates the light intensity.

XL-Loft

This 2,600-square-foot loft in a former factory is composed of a number of different spaces, each with its own depth, height, and ambience. A central box contains the bedroom and dressing room, which can be closed off from adjacent rooms; a 52-foot-long glass wall delineates the kitchen/dining area, storage room, and bathroom; a 69-foot-long wall of bookshelves cuts across the loft space; a 46-foot-long loggia distinguishes the office from the living room and kitchen/dining room.

Architect: Nico Heysse
Location: Brussels, Belgium
Date of construction: 2005
Photography: Laurent Brandajs

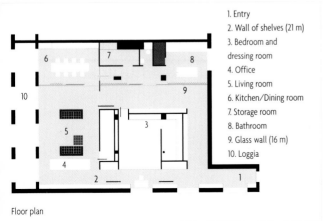

1. Entry
2. Wall of shelves (21 m)
3. Bedroom and dressing room
4. Office
5. Living room
6. Kitchen/Dining room
7. Storage room
8. Bathroom
9. Glass wall (16 m)
10. Loggia

Floor plan

A 52-foot-long glass wall and a 69-foot-long wall of bookshelves create dramatic perspectives in this loft, located in a district of the Belgian capital.

Walking through the loft,
the visitor slowly
discovers the structure
of the floor plan and
experiences different
sensations of depth
and perspective.

Each space in this loft has its own character. A system of panel doors closes off the cool, white bedroom from adjacent spaces where there is more color and more activity.

The hallways of this loft have been deliberately kept wide so the original dimension of the loft space can be appreciated from a number of different places.

44

A black box under a lowered
ceiling accommodates
the bathing area,
made more interesting with
mood lighting.

Architect: Julie Richards
Architectural Design
Location: London, U.K.
Date of construction: 2001
Photography: A. Butler/
Photofoyer

This residence was designed with the rapidly changing role of modern living spaces in mind. The aim was to create a series of multifunctional spaces that can be reinvented easily. Responding to functions oscillating between life and work, flexible vertical partitions were used as barriers separating the public and private areas. These partitions give a different sense of spatiality depending on their location.

45

Vertical partitions separate the public from the private areas. The sunken public area further contrasts the horizontal with the vertical lines of the loft.

1. Living area
2. Kitchen
3. Dining area
4. Office
5. Bedroom
6. Bathroom
7. WC

Floor plan

46

The visual, tactile, and luminescent qualities of the materials used emphasize the division between public and private spaces.

Perry Street

The design of this West Village apartment—once "sad, banal, and dreary" say the architects—centers around a single storage wall, which divides the public from the private space. The wall has 12-foot-tall pocket doors of translucent plastic and poplar; when open the doors which allow each area to blend into the other. The hall closet and shower room are hidden from view behind a wall of white lacquered panels.

Architect: Messana O'Rorke
Architects
Location: New York, NY, U.S.A.
Date of construction: 2005
Photography: Elizabeth Felicella

Floor plan

1. Hall
2. Hall closet
3. Shower room
4. Kitchen
5. Dining area
6. Living area
7. Storage wall
8. Master bedroom
9. Master bathroom
10. Master closet
11. Guest bedroom

An existing concrete column defines the entry hall and separates it from the living room beyond, which centers around an existing fireplace.

48

A series of exposed and
obscured dimmable
fluorescent light fixtures
bring bright daylight-quality
light into the space's
darkest corners.

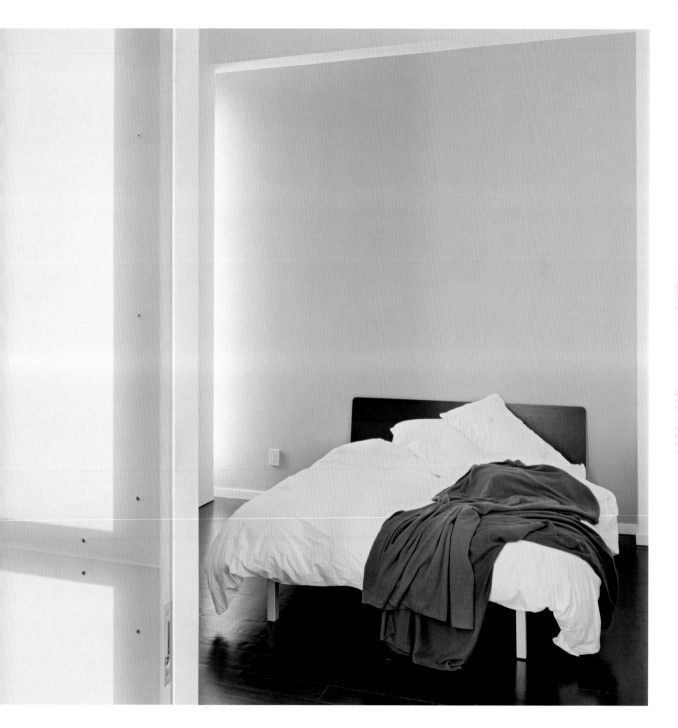

Architect's Loft

The architect of this loft transformed a former manufacturing space in the New York City district of Hell's Kitchen into a home for himself. Juxtaposing modern updates with vintage furnishings, the architect managed to create a contemporary living space. A freestanding maple wall separates the private zone from the entertainment area and a green gypsum partition differentiates the main living area from the kitchen and bathing areas.

Architect: Steve E. Blatz
Location: New York, NY, U.S.A.
Date of construction: 2002
Photography: Sur Press Agencia

49

The industrial urban
neighborhood of New
York's Hell's Kitchen
contrasts with the calm
minimal architecture
and furnishings.

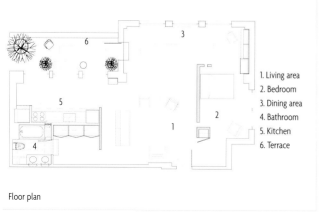

1. Living area
2. Bedroom
3. Dining area
4. Bathroom
5. Kitchen
6. Terrace

Floor plan

Steel windows let in abundant light, and the original concrete floor grids are duplicated on the face of the maple wall (see following pages).

The maple wall embraces the sleeping area and gives it a sense of privacy and enclosure without turning it into a formal bedroom.

Single-Family Loft

This 5,500-square-foot loft apartment is located in the historic Montgomery Ward building, which was constructed in 1908 and designed to follow the flow of the Chicago River. The lower level of this building once fit 24 railcars end to end. The expansive spatial qualities of the original building are preserved, as well as the bell-capped columns and large steel windows.

Architect: Vincent James
Associates Architects
Location: Chicago, IL, U.S.A.
Date of construction: 2005
Photography: Michael Moran

A palette of hickory wood
paneling and plaster walls
is employed to complement
the relationship with the
original board-formed
concrete slabs
and concrete columns.

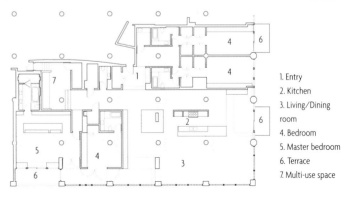

1. Entry
2. Kitchen
3. Living/Dining
room
4. Bedroom
5. Master bedroom
6. Terrace
7. Multi-use space

Main level plan

Loft Nollet

Architect: Daniel Linze, Pascale
Lacroix (interior architect),
Tecla Tangorra (designer)
Location: Anderlecht, Belgium
Date of construction: 2005
Photography: Laurent Brandajs

The basic concept for the design of this loft was based on some elementary
principles. First because it is located on a ground floor, the space had to be
protected from the exterior. It was also important to maintain the feeling
of the volume as a whole, yet create truly isolated rooms. The original elements of
the space had to be emphasized, and the design had to take advantage of the high
ceilings. The architects did so by creating mezzanines.

1. Living area
2. Kitchen/Dining area
3. Bedroom
4. Bathroom
5. Laundry room/Boiler room
6. WC
7. Mezzanine

Ground floor

Mezzanine

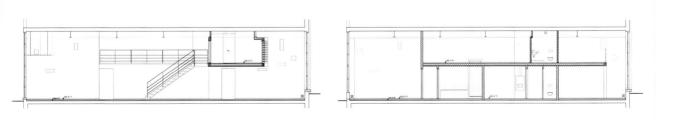

Sections

This loft contains two
functional areas—a kitchen
and an office—suspended
from the ceiling. This
creates contradictions and
delimitings particular zones.

The suspended box is deliberately very low (close to the ground floor) to dramatize the passage between the living room and kitchen/dining room.

The private spaces—the
bedrooms and bathrooms—
are isolated from the
open-plan space on
the ground floor.

Loft Lloydkwartier

Located in a former warehouse facing Rotterdam harbor, the main characteristic of this loft is its spaciousness. To maintain this quality, two separate modules were created for the bedrooms and the children's room and placed in the open space. The bedrooms are half sunken into the floor and clad in natural stone to reflect the waters of the quay. The functionality of the children's bedroom is expanded with a cupboard hidden behind brilliant cloth-covered panels.

Architect: 123DV architectuur
& consult
Location: Rotterdam,
The Netherlands
Date of construction: 2005
Photography: Christiaan de Bruijne

56

A hidden cupboard works as an extension of the children's bedroom and the padded panels present themselves as a toy within the open space.

1. Entrance hall
2. WC
3. Bathroom
4. Living area
5. Children's bedroom an hidden cupboard
6. Play and storage room
7. Bedroom

Ground floor

The roof of the bedroom doubles as more living space—a platform with a built-in kitchen and a whirlpool bath that overlooks the harbor.

1. Kitchen
2. Dining area
3. Whirlpool bath
4. Living area
5. Children's bedroom and hidden cupboard
6. Play and storage room

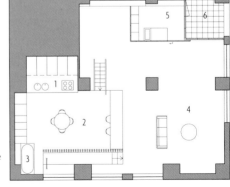

First floor

Nomad House

The starting point for this home in Madrid was light. Not an abundance of it, rather light as found in Scandinavian homes, where it remains a subtle, pale, gray element. The home of a young couple without children at the moment, the space to be versatile and future changes had to be possible without having to carry out any kinds of construction. Moreover, the concept had to be simple at a functional level, so the architects created a system in which absolutely everything is mobile.

Architect: **Stone Designs**
Location: **Madrid, Spain**
Date of construction: **2006**
Photography: **Juan Merinero**

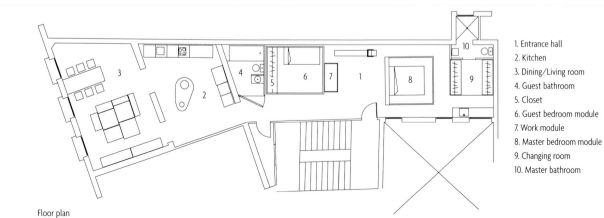

1. Entrance hall
2. Kitchen
3. Dining/Living room
4. Guest bathroom
5. Closet
6. Guest bedroom module
7. Work module
8. Master bedroom module
9. Changing room
10. Master bathroom

Floor plan

The designers' characteristic graphic elements play an important part in the interior design of this home, which emulates a natural environment.

WHERE WE
EAT

WHERE YOU
DREAM

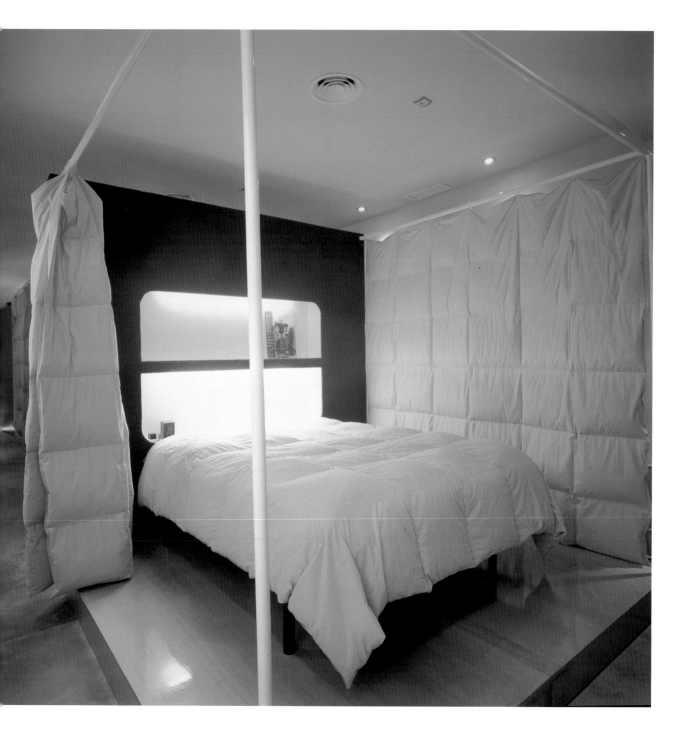

59

The guest bedroom and main bedroom are appropriately closed off with a curtain of duvets, which hang from a 1.18-inch metal pipe.

60

The concept in terms of
function was very simple:
Absolutely everything had
to be mobile, turning every
room of the house into a
modular space.

61

A wooden platform 4in
off the ground holds a bed
and helps create a cozy
atmosphere behind a
series of duvets
used as curtains.

Loft Gleimstrasse

The architects call this an unfolded cocoon for an open mind. The loft is a rooftop
addition to a typical nineteenth-century building in the trendy part of Berlin.
It incorporates a peculiar "Mega-Form," which hides intimate spaces such as the
bathrooms and even the staircases and storage rooms. This dense central block
leaves plenty of open surrounding space with infinite possibilities.

Architect: Graft
Location: Berlin, Germany
Date of construction: 2004
Photography: Jan Bitter

A sculptural Mega-Form hides and integrates private spaces and is a perfect solution to create space and storage.

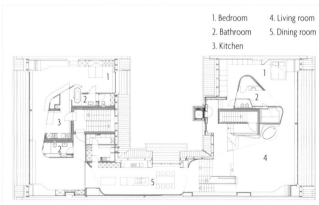

1. Bedroom 4. Living room
2. Bathroom 5. Dining room
3. Kitchen

Floor plan

A kind of playground is created around a dense central block, thus providing numerous combinations of atmospheres and functions.

Loft for Two Artists

The architects of this loft wanted to create a juxtaposition of folkloric elements with an open and modern spatial approach. The clients—a painter and a sculptor—wanted their home to bear elements of the Mexican culture. A tear-dropped sculptural element dominates the main living space and integrates kitchen storage and appliances. It recalls the colors and handicraft traditions of Mexico, where the owners spend several months a year.

Architect: Aardvarchitecture
Location: New York, NY, U.S.A.
Date of construction: 2004
Photography: Paúl Rivera/
Arch Photo

64

Enormous folding doors
feature inset magnifying
lenses that focus light and
blur the view from one side
of the doors to the other.

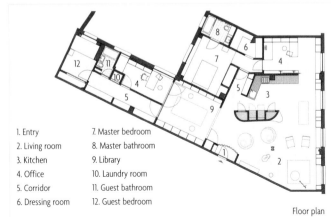

1. Entry	7. Master bedroom
2. Living room	8. Master bathroom
3. Kitchen	9. Library
4. Office	10. Laundry room
5. Corridor	11. Guest bathroom
6. Dressing room	12. Guest bedroom

Floor plan

65

Large west-facing windows
provide both beautiful
afternoon light and
the backdrop to a series of
display niches for the
sculptor's work.

Orange Egg

The conditions in this bright second-floor loft were ideal for realizing the proposed aims of the design: fluidity, dynamism, versatility, and making the kitchen the most important element. A central egg-shaped closed space containing the bathroom and kitchen was created, making the latter the focus of the home. The other spaces in the apartment flow fluidly around this oval, but the space can be easily tranformed into whatever is needed at the time.

Architect: **Lucía Borrego Gómez-Pallete**
Location: **Madrid, Spain**
Date of construction: **2004**
Photography: **Jordi Canosa**

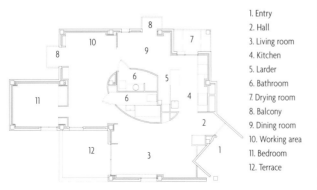

1. Entry
2. Hall
3. Living room
4. Kitchen
5. Larder
6. Bathroom
7. Drying room
8. Balcony
9. Dining room
10. Working area
11. Bedroom
12. Terrace

Floor plan

The "egg" containing the service areas is the central element of the home and the rest of the spaces flow naturally around this structure.

67

Windows carved into the structure allow light to enter the bathrooms and let the user look out to the living and dining area, without others being able to look in.

Old Textile Mill

In 1998, Tilman Paas bought this former textile mill outside Cologne. When he discovered this hidden jewel, it was in a state of disrepair. He restored the building, conserving as much as possible of the original design and materials and he rented out creatively designed lofts, offices, and showrooms to companies. He held on to the boiler house, with its 213-foot-chimney, and now used it as his own living-working space.

Architect: **Tilman Paas**
Location: **Euskirchen, Germany**
Date of construction: **2003**
Photography: **Chiesa/Photofoyer**

68

Modern, functional, and beautiful components easily work together with the original industrial layout and materials in the bolier house of this former textile mill.

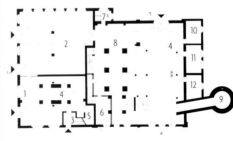

Ground floor

1. Garage
2. Workshop
3. Stairs/Hallway
4. Storage room
5. Electric room
6. Heating room
7. WC
8. Workshop/Storage room
9. Chimney
10. Recreation room
11. Social room
12. Dressing room

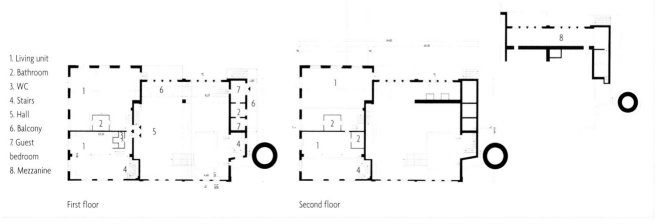

1. Living unit
2. Bathroom
3. WC
4. Stairs
5. Hall
6. Balcony
7. Guest bedroom
8. Mezzanine

First floor

Second floor

69

The bathrooms and toilets
are concealed in a double
cube, which looks like
a simple bookcase
from the front.

1. Workshop
2. Living unit
3. WC
4. Bathroom
5. Steel stairs

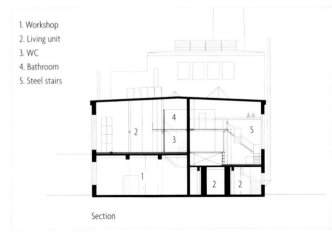

Section

Levels

Finley Apartment

Architect: AvroKO
Location: New York, NY, U.S.A.
Date of construction: 2005
Photography: Michael Weber,
Yuki Kuwana

Redefining the urban residential environment through their smart.space project, the architects of this apartment combined lifestyle architecture with traditional architecture. The result is a spacious triplex with environmentally sound construction materials and a stylish design, that encourages social interaction and organization. This example of beautiful and healthy urban living can be applied to an infinite variety of dwellings worldwide.

70

Moving from the kitchen to
the main living room and on
to the upper level, one can
sense the unity and flow
throughout this triplex.

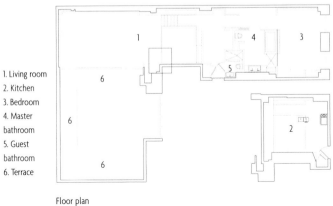

1. Living room
2. Kitchen
3. Bedroom
4. Master
bathroom
5. Guest
bathroom
6. Terrace

Floor plan

71

One of the main features
of the apartment is
seamless, large-scale
metamorphosing elements
for space efficiency.

72

Environmentally sound
construction materials
and a stylish design
encourage organization
and social interaction
throughout this loft.

73

A combination of technical wit with creative élan, and lifestyle architecture with traditional architecture makes for a prototypical urban living space.

Loft Via Maiocchi

Architect: Fabio Azzolina
Location: Milan, Italy
Date of construction: 2006
Photography: Andrea
Martiradonna

This former carpentry workshop in a Milanese courtyard proves that there are no limits to the creation of loft homes in spaces that were previously designated for other uses. This L-shaped building opens onto a garden, and the interiors have been organized around it. The ground level is reserved for living and service areas and is connected to the mezzanine level via light metal and wooden stairs, which accentuate the verticality of the space.

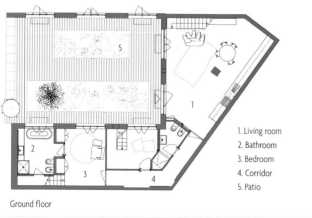

Ground floor

1. Living room
2. Bathroom
3. Bedroom
4. Corridor
5. Patio

74

A suspended staircase in the living room leads to an office mezzanine. Large sliding doors blend the indoor with the outdoor spaces and make the room seem bigger.

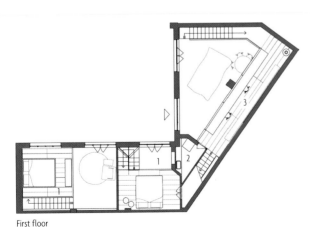

First floor

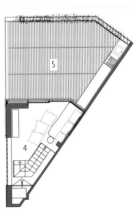

Mezzanine

1. Bedroom
2. Laundry room
3. Office
4. Relaxation room
5. Terrace

75

The bathrooms, clad in mosaic tiles and illuminated by back-lit mirrors, are located beneath the double-height bedrooms on the mezzanine level.

Loft in 13th Century Church

A former thirteenth-century church with frescoes dating back to the fourteenth-century has been carefully transformed into a cozy family home. To leave the space as intact as possible and make the most of the height of the space (9 m), three attics were created on different levels, each representing a domestic area.

Architect: Francesco Donnaloia/
Spacestudio
Location: Florence, Italy
Date of construction: 2000
Photography: A. Pecchio/
Photofoyer

76

White shelves made of plaster are built into the edges of the space and make their way up through the three floors to fulfill their function in each space.

Triangular brackets
supporting the levels also
help maintain the space
clean and clear without the
need for pillars.

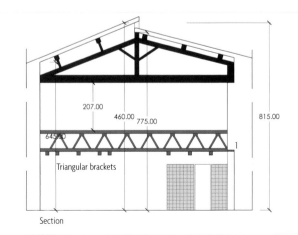

207.00
460.00 775.00
815.00
645.00

Triangular brackets

Section

Loft Gerald S

This loft in Berlin was redesigned to provide more storage space. The architects decided to accentuate the spatial continuity and installed a series of ribbonlike panels along the wall to visually link the main areas. At the same time, these panels successfully hide, hold, and store a myriad small items. These inconspicuous, wall-mounted units are actually off-the-shelf IKEA storage boxes, framed by custom joinery.

Architect: **Raum:team 92**
Location: **Berlin, Germany**
Date of construction: **2005**
Photography: **Stefan Meyer**

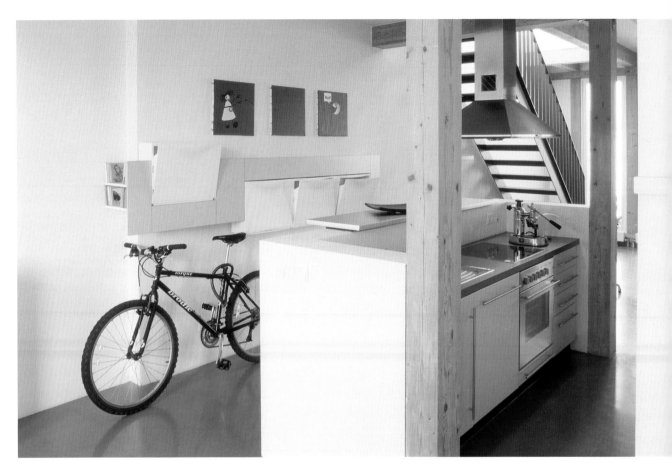

Custom-made joinery
frames the kitchen area and
windows on the lower level.

79

Attractive and useful storage units were incorporated into the design of this loft to help solve a storage problem.

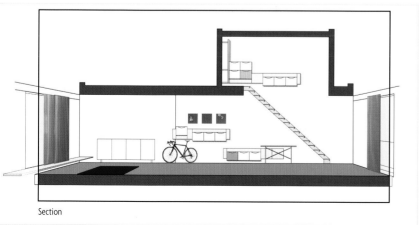

Section

80

Bold color accents within the loft reference existing and new furniture, such as the low seats along the window wall, the sofa, and the light fixtures.

Art Lovers' Loft

Situated in Palermo Viejo, a trendy neighborhood in Buenos Aires, the former Minetti Flour Mills (Molinos Harineros Minetti) was transformed into a building of lofts in 1992-1993. In search of a home with a garden not too far from the city—a rarity in many big cities—the owners got lucky when they found this gem. They converted the space into a contemporary urban loft that reflects their love of art.

Architect: Fernando Entin
Location: Buenos Aires, Argentina
Date of construction: 2000
Photography: Sur Press Agencia

Initially the decor this loft reflected Santa Fe style, but it was completely redecorated and given a contemporary urban look.

The owners' personality is reflected in their home: They started a small collection of contemporary art, which they incorporated into the interior design of their house.

Felkner Loft

The couple who owns this 2,500-square-foot live-work space wanted to continue an urban lifestyle within the context of a typical Southern California suburban neighborhood. Large-scale volumes contrast with more intimate studies of body sensuality. Architectural details provide a level of intimacy in each space, while contrasting materials ignite the human desire to experience through touch. The relationship between body and ritual is intensified in each of the bathing rooms.

Architect: Luce et Studio Architects
Location: San Diego, CA, U.S.A.
Date of construction: 2005
Photography: A. Butler/ Photofoyer

The roughness of exposed
concrete walls contrasts
with the smooth and
elegant wooden panels
and flooring and the opaque
glass separators.

84

The juxtaposition of the sculptural staircase's smooth and rough materials marks the choreography of the body's movement through space.

85

The body is most
vulnerable in the bathing
areas (next pages):
Voyeuristic aspects of
transparency meet a
secret box where metal
touches the skin.

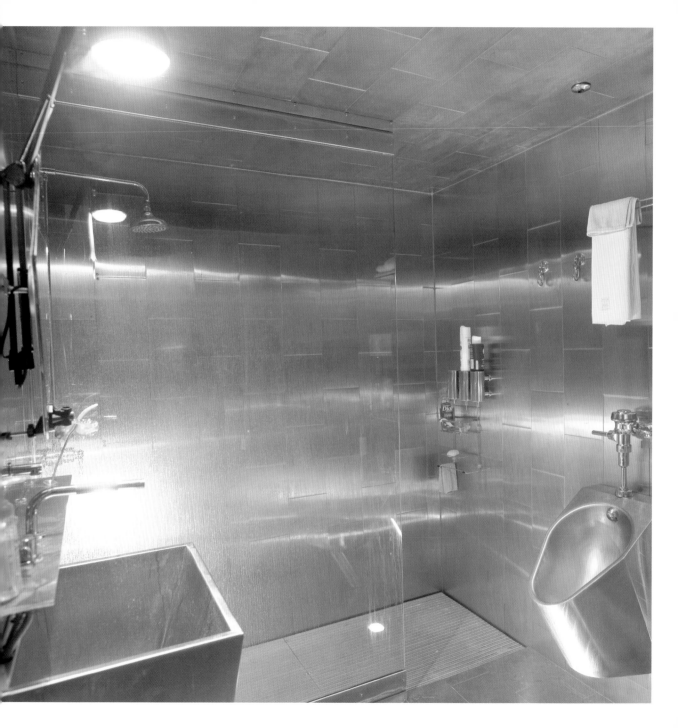

Loft O'Shea

A typical Buenos Aires "PH" (terraced town houses each with an interior patio, connected by a corridor) was refurbished as a loft. Facing the interior patio, the ground floor living areas—including the living room, kitchen, small office area—and the TV room on a mezzanine level are united into one large and bright space.

Architect: Rodrigo Cunill, Juana Grichener, Patricia O'Shea
Location: Buenos Aires, Argentina
Date of construction: 2004
Photography: Sur Press Agencia

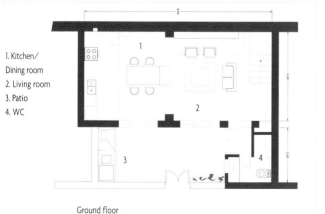

1. Kitchen/
Dining room
2. Living room
3. Patio
4. WC

Ground floor

An open fireplace is the centerpiece of the ground floor and divides element between the kitchen and living areas. A staircase leads from the living room to the first floor (next pages).

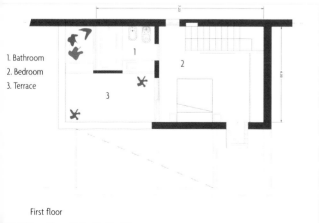

1. Bathroom
2. Bedroom
3. Terrace

First floor

The Shipping News

Here, inner-city industrial building with Manhattan proportions has been turned into the home of a maritime consultant. Though not obvious, a nautical feeling is nonetheless present. The owner's maritime connections are suggested in the gangway with white railings and exposed trusses, while the building's industrial past and a touch of urban élan are also reflected in this sparse yet dynamic home.

Architect: Greg Meagher, Simon Croft/Fusion (designer)
Location: Cape Town, South Africa
Date of construction: 2005
Photography: Keith Bernstein/Inside

87

Urban chic meets a
sparse industrial space.
The owner's personal tastes
and elements of his
occupation are incorporated
into the design of this
Cape Town loft.

1. Entrance hall
2. Office
3. Dining room
4. Kitchen
5. Living room
6. Pool
7. Deck
8. Bathroom
9. Bedroom
10. Dressing room
11. Storage room
12. Home entertainment

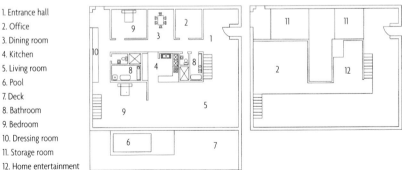

Ground floor

Mezzanine

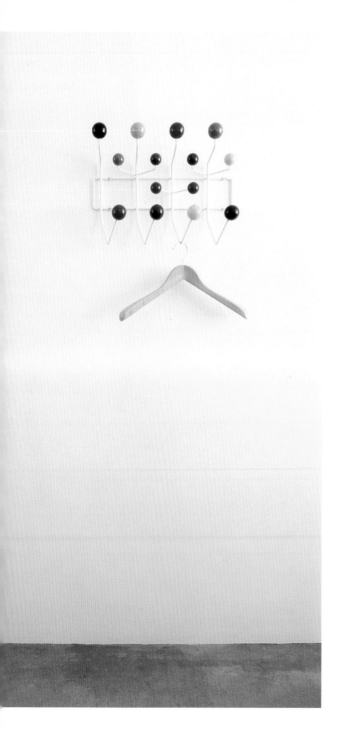

Loft in Lyon

Architect: Jacques Chevalier
Location: Lyon, France
Date of construction: 1999
Photography: Erick Saillet/Inside

To take advantage of this sprawling industrial space, several levels were built, accommodating different living quarters on each floor. Large windows, a minimum amount of furniture and an open stairwell help maintain a spacious feeling throughout the loft. A collection of antiques works surprisingly well in combination with exposed wooden beams and industrial elements.

88

Pieces of antique furniture—
not usually associated with
contemporary lofts—take on
a primary role in this large,
light-suffused urban loft.

Private areas are visually
separated from the rest of
the loft's open-plan layout.
The type and color of
flooring defines each area.

Interno/Esterno

A nineteenth-century military building in the heart of Milan's Navigli district has been converted into a series of dwellings designed in the *casa di ringhiera* style—multistory buildings with doors leading onto a common balcony. Part of the ground floor, the former stables of a barrack, is now a 2,153-square-foot loft apartment for a young Milanese entrepreneur.

Architect: G. Longo, A. Palmarini,
I. Rebosio, F. Spagnulo/Studio A
Location: Milan, Italy
Date of construction: 2000
Photography: Andrea Martiradonna

1. Entry
2. Living room
3. Dining room
4. Office
5. Kitchen
6. Bathroom
7. Bathtub

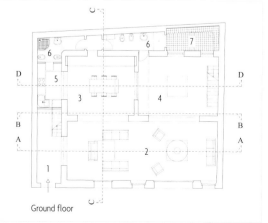

Ground floor

90

Two mezzanine floors have been created in this huge space. Windows and a walkway connect the bedroom, study, and library on the mezzanine with the central space.

91

The doorway arches characteristic of this building have been preserved in the design to heighten the marvelous sense of space.

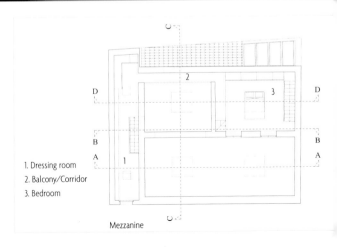

1. Dressing room
2. Balcony/Corridor
3. Bedroom

Mezzanine

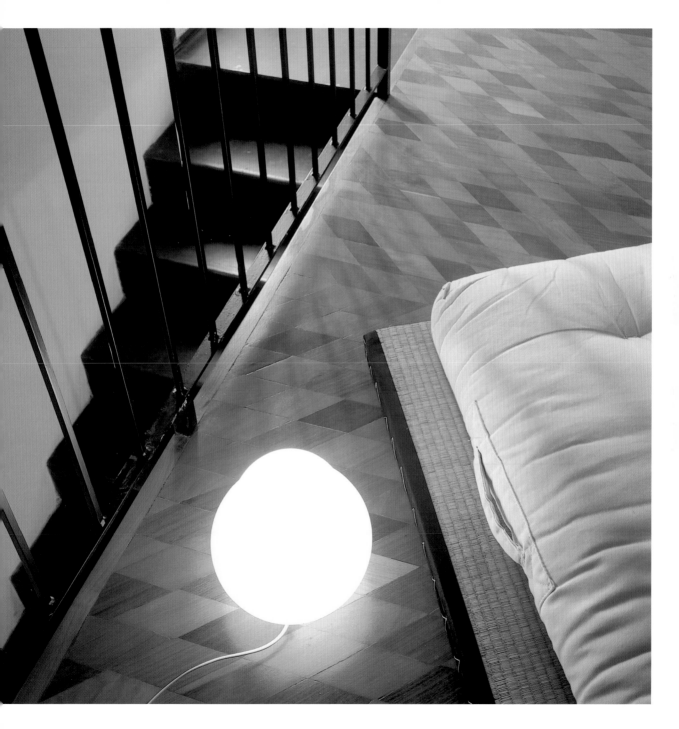

Loft Cramer

Outdoor living—camping in the open air—served as the inspiration for the interior architecture of this loft. The owners wanted to reflect the idea of relaxation using outdoor materials indoors. The place is also inspired by the many travels, objects, and ideas brought back from their trips, which they try to apply to their daily lives, such as the ladder leading to the upper level, which is inspired by a trip one summer to the lush and wild Delta del Tigre islands.

Architect: Mauro Bernardini,
Martín Churba (interior designer)
Location: Buenos Aires, Argentina
Date of construction: 2004
Photography: Sur Press Agencia

92

The interior design of this urban loft is inspired by the owners' many travels and their love of outdoor living.

One of the owners made an original chair enrobed in old belts (donated by friends), which complements the other elements collected on the owners' travels.

94

Small windows—similar to those in mosquito nets— have been cut out of the curtains to offer a more romantic view of the surrounding landscape.

95

After once spending hours on a dock in the Delta del Tigre islands, the owners came back with a design for their stairs.

Shepherdess Walk

This loft is one of 30 apartments in a converted Victorian clothing factory in Shoreditch, London. The owner was exposed to the loft scene in SoHo, New York, where he lived for a time. When he returned to London, he sought a loft in a former industrial space. The main priorities for its design were space, light, atmosphere, and being able to live and work in the same space.

Architect: Niki Turner Designs
Location: Shoreditch, U.K.
Date of construction: 2003
Photography: Spaceworks.org

96

To help keep the space as open and light as possible, sliding, sound-blasted Perspex screens were used to separate the private areas.

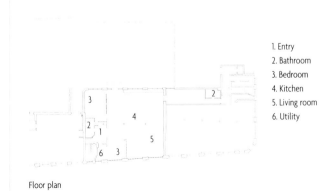

1. Entry
2. Bathroom
3. Bedroom
4. Kitchen
5. Living room
6. Utility

Floor plan

97

The priorities in creating
this loft were space, light,
atmosphere, and design.
The dining area furnishings
epitomize that mission.

Transparency

Former Collet Buildings

The decorator of this home has carefully chosen furnishings to reflect the history of the building (it had been a commercial bakery), while maintaining the volume and spaciousness to create a comfortable, contemporary, and urban dwelling. Daylight floods the space thanks to a number of skylights, and the generous use of glass and the color white.

Interior designer: Eugénie Collet
Location: Brussels, Belgium
Date of construction: 2004
Photography: Serge Anton/Inside

98

Original structures
combined with antique
furnishings and decor
and vintage work in
harmony with modern
elements to create a
contemporary home.

Sunlight streams into the sprawling rustic kitchen through an enormous skylight. Cabinets line the walls, and marble tops a professional-size work island.

Urban Heritage

This couple, both environmental architects turned a Cape Town warehouse that had been a landmark since 1904 into an eco-friendly home. The space is split into two zones: private spaces—bedrooms and bathrooms—and a public space with a vast living-dining-kitchen area at the core. A central open-air courtyard was also built to let in more air and light. Wooden floors and simple shelving complement the dominant feature: exposed ceiling beams.

Architect: Wolf & Wolf Architects
Location: Cape Town, South Africa
Date of construction: 2006
Photography: Martin Hahn/Inside

100

A Victorian bath tub was
re-enameled in orange,
which complements the
honey-colored bamboo
and wood ceiling as well as
giving the place a
touch of color.

Loft Maluquer

Architect: Gianni Ruggiero
Location: Barcelona, Spain
Date of construction: 2002
Photography: Jordi Miralles

This 1,830-square-foot space was originally a ground-floor parking garage. Due to its trapezoidal floor plan, barely two sides faced the exterior. It fell to the architect to find a way of transforming this dark, damp, and abandoned space into a livable home. To avoid opening up the home to passersby on the street side, the architect decided to open up the heart of the home by creating an inner patio.

101

To convert a former ground-floor parking garage into a modern home with a fish-bowl style interior, a patio was built in the center to let in plenty of daylight.

1. Entry
2. Living/Dining room/Kitchen
3. Patio
4. Bedroom
5. Bathroom/Dressing room
6. WC
7. Study
8. Laundry room

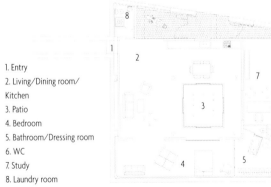

Floor plan

102

An exposed-brick wall
resembling an outdoor
wall runs the length of
the large living-kitchen-
dining area, uniting these
zones in the process.

103

Large sliding doors or
windows close off
or open up the bedroom,
the entryway, the study, and
zones of the bathroom,
according to need.

Windsor Loft

The design of this former neon-sign factory and printing workshop reflects architectural strategies in modern residential spaces within an urban context. An inner courtyard creates continuity and a visual communication between the private and the public domains. A cruciform-shaped column in the middle of the living areas is testament to the home's industrial past and helps divide the open-plan layout.

Architect: Architects EAT
Location: Windsor, Victoria, Australia
Date of construction: 2006
Photography: Shania Shegedyn, John Gollings, Jason Reekie

Ranks of floor tiles and recessed lighting tracks help define the entertainment, dining, lounging, and circulation areas on the open first floor.

1. Patio
2. Kitchen
3. Entertaining, dining, sitting and circulation area
4. Master bedroom
5. Master bathroom
6. Guest bedroom
7. Guest bathroom

Floor plan

The only facade facing the
street contains a reference
to the place's history: red,
patterned, glow-in-the-dark
plastic framing a window.

The courtyard plays an important role in connecting the private and public areas. The bedroom and bathroom are visually associated with the main living areas.

Casa Cachée

Two new industrial-like house-ateliers (and an office building) were erected on the site of an abandoned garage and some old and unappealing buildings. This loft is situated in the most isolated part of the site. A patio surrounded by glass and polycarbonate panels ensures that the home is awash in light during the day and creates a feeling of spaciousness for the couple living here with their children.

Architect: Barthélemy-Ifrah
Location: Colombes, France
Date of construction: 2003
Photography: Mathieu Lesavre

1. Entry
2. WC
3. Kitchen
4. Living room
5. Patio
6. Bathroom
7. Bedroom
8. Laundry room
9. Office
10. Master bedroom
11. Master bathroom
12. Playroom

Ground floor

First floor

107

Though the original buildings were knocked down, the new construction pays homage to the site's industrial past and uses raw industrial materials in its design.

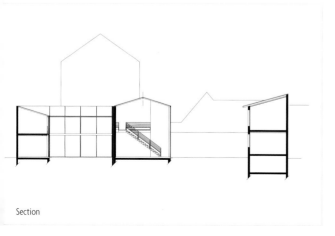

Section

108

Interior and exterior can be
confused in the patio's huge
alternating glass and
polycarbonate panels.

The main principles for the
design were volume and
light; the rest naturally fell
into place, except two low
walls and the staircase.

Fifth Garden Loft

Architect: Law Ling Kit,
Virginia Lung/One Plus
Partnership
Location: Shenzhen, China
Date of construction: 2005
Photography: Virginia Lung

The client of this loft in China wanted to reflect the Chinese aesthetic in the interior design. The designers chose deep pink, the color of plum blossoms, instead of red, which is the color most often tied to Chinese style. The main challenge? To avoid the feminine stereotype associated with the color pink, and instead to create a space that exudes calm and elegance.

110

Lots of black and grey and simple and straight lines were used throughout the loft to help bring out the glamour of the color pink.

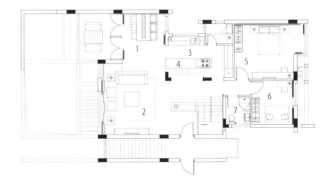

1. Dining room
2. Living room
3. Kitchen
4. Breakfast area
5. Parents' bedroom
6. Childen's bedroom
7. Bathroom

Ground floor

111

The color of plum blossoms, deep pink is difficult to use in interior design, though combining it with darker colors accentuates its elegant side.

1. Master bathroom
2. Master bedroom
3. Bedroom
4. Study

First floor

112

The colors black and white were used in other rooms, such as the guest bedroom, where the ambience is calm.

Raw and Urban

A chocolate factory—with huge industrial spaces, an inner courtyard, an enormous chimney, and a village atmosphere—located in the Lxelles neighborhood of Brussels was transformed to accommodate a series of lofts ranging from 1,615- and 4,306-square-feet. Each of the twelve lofts was designed according to the needs and means of each occupant, thus creating a variety of styles: raw and industrial, artistic, minimalist, and chic.

Architect: **Damien de Halleux**
Location: **Brussels, Belgium**
Date of construction: **2003**
Photography: **Serge Anton/Inside**

113

Shelves of recycled
industrial wood were used
to create a custom
bookcase for this living area
to underscored the loft's
raw and urban look.

Paunero House

Architect: Javier Rivarola, Gustavo
Trosman, Ricardo Norton/
RTN Architects
Location: Buenos Aires, Argentina
Date of construction: 2000
Photography: Sur Press Agencia

Located in the suburbs of Buenos Aires, this family home is one in a trilogy of houses based on one design concept. A glass-walled interior patio is the core of the house: All rooms on the lower and upper levels are organized around this open space. This interior void visually connects the entire home—horizontally, diagonally, and vertically—and lets the outdoors into the house.

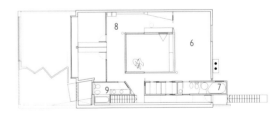

Lower level

1. Entry
2. Library
3. Living/Dining area
4. Patio
5. Kitchen/Dining area

Upper level

6. Master bedroom
7. Master bathroom
8. Bedroom
9. Bathroom

A wooden bookcase that extends to the top of the upper floor runs the entire length of a dividing wall.

Longitudinal section

115

A metal horizontal volume,
which houses the
bathroom, contrasts with
the verticality of the home.

Loft in Bagnolet

Architect: Pierre Bragnier
Location: Bagnolet (Paris), France
Date of construction: 2003
Photography: Antoine
Baralhe/Inside

This contemporary home successfully incorporates the concept of a loft. An open-plan layout brings the living, dining, and relaxation areas together in one space, while a glass bridge connects the private areas on the upper level both to the space below and to the exterior courtyard. The bridge also adds an industrial element to this otherwise very modern and stylish home.

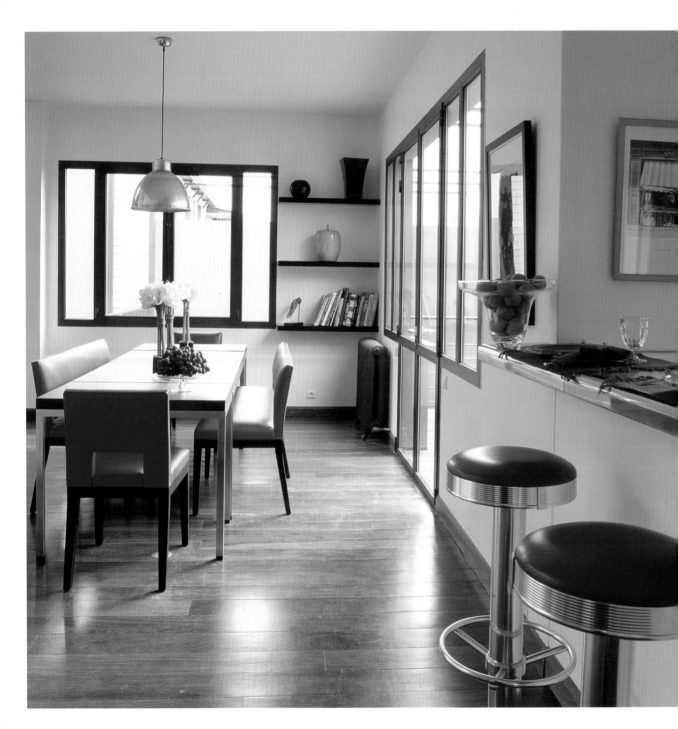

116

A dash of red in the kitchen
and dining areas helps
identify these spaces within
the open-plan layout.

The bedroom connects to
the rest of the house via a
glass pathway, which also
leads to the exterior.

Loft facing Eiffel Tower

Architect: Serge Caillaud,
C. Dubosq (stylist)
Location: Paris, France
Date of construction: 2005
Photography: Stephen
Clément/Inside

The panoramic views are undoubtedly the most impressive feature of this top-floor apartment in the French capital. A skylight in the dining-living area ensures that as much light as possible reaches the interior—even on the grayest of days. Curtains and glass separators conceal the more private areas, when necessary.

One room easily flows into
the next, thanks to the
open-plan layout of this loft.
Venetian blinds provide
privacy and create a
cozy atmosphere.

119

The flooring in the bedroom differs from that in the rest of the space. Closing the curtains around this area makes for an intimate nocturnal space.

One of Paris's most emblematic structures is perfectly framed in the master bedroom and bathroom windows.

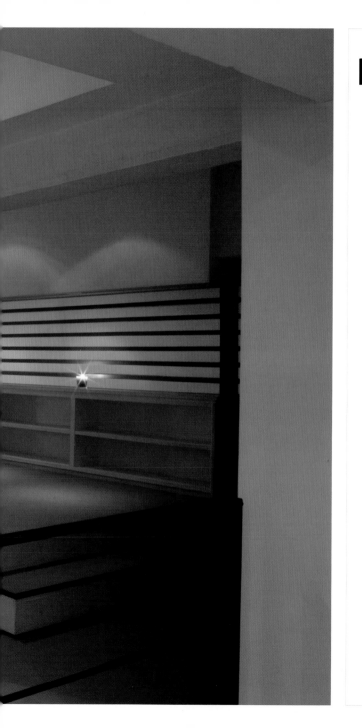

Not Just Industrial Spaces

Parragon House

Originally a school in South London, this building was converted into a home for a Swedish couple who were looking for an uncompromisingly modern interior that would suppress all extraneous details in a completely sleek and minimalist design. To make the most of the full height and the windows, a mezzanine level and a suspended corridor were built to house the bedroom and storage space.

Architect: **Nico Rensch/ Architeam**
Location: **London, U.K.**
Date of construction: **2000**
Photo: **Adam Butler/Photofoyer**

A kitchen unit is hidden
behind doors in a built-in
cupboard. When closed,
the unit neatly blends into
the space.

Loft in a 15th Century Palace

Architect: Lorena Luccioni
Location: Filottrano, Italy
Date of construction: 2003
Photography: Alessandro Ciampi

This home design adheres to the concept of a loft, but not entirely. Rather, individual rooms have been laid out in a loft style: The living areas, nearest to the home's entrance, are articulated on two levels, and the night area is separated by sliding doors. The original structural elements of this fifteenth-century palace were maintained and combined with completely new elements using modern materials.

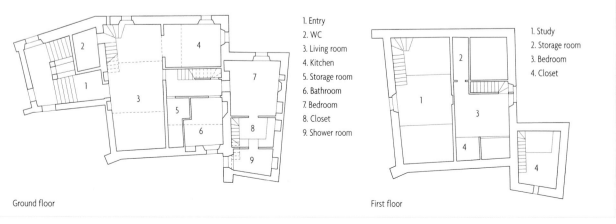

1. Entry
2. WC
3. Living room
4. Kitchen
5. Storage room
6. Bathroom
7. Bedroom
8. Closet
9. Shower room

1. Study
2. Storage room
3. Bedroom
4. Closet

Ground floor

First floor

122

Set in a fifteenth century palace, a new, extremely articulated home has been created. Doors on wheels separate day areas from night areas.

This Dutch water tower, which dates from 1931, was converted into an unparalled twenty-first-century home spread over nine levels. The architects faced many challenges: letting more daylight in; strengthening the relationship with the back courtyard, maintaining the interior's industrial characteristics; and in the tower, ensuring an effective, efficient layout for several small round rooms that lay one on top of the other, while preserving the tower's spaciousness.

Soest Water Tower

Architect: Zecc Architecten
Location: Soest,
The Netherlands
Date of construction: 2004
Photography: Jeroen Musch

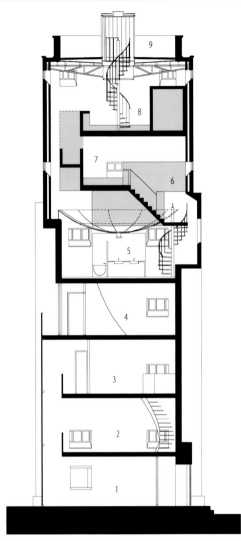

1. Entry/Kitchen
2. Living room
3. Playroom/Guest bedroom
4. Children's bedroom
5. Bathroom

6. Sauna
7. Parents' live and work area
8. Parents' bedroom
9. Roof terrace

Section

The steel bottom of the original water reservoir divides the tower space in half. The bottom, with the bathroom, living room, and children's room, is mainly reserved for daytime use.

1. Entry/Kitchen
2. Living room
3. Playroom/Guest bedroom
4. Children's bedroom
5. Bathroom
6. Sauna
7. Parents' live and work area
8. Parents' bedroom
9. Roof terrace

Floor plans

123

By exteriorizing the three-story-high facade, the architects created a void so that different levels can be openly connected.

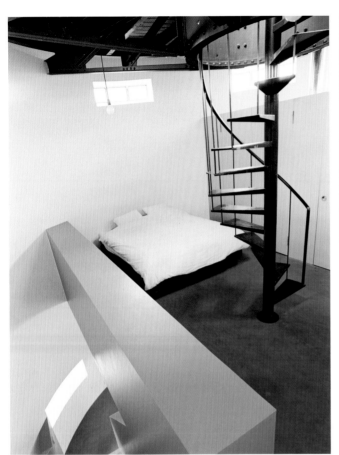

124

Angular volumes for sleeping, working, and reading functions built into the original water reservoir underscore the cylindrical shape.

The Y Apartment

A former basketball court and suspended running track, once part of a YMCA, have been spectacularly converted into a luxurious loft. The rawness of the place was preserved and the original floorboards, which were laid down over five decades ago, were maintained to give this residence a unique touch and respect its history.

Architect: The Apartment
Creative Agency
Location: New York, NY, U.S.A.
Date of construction: 2005
Photography: Michael Weber

125

Original elements alluding
to the place's past are
preserved, and they
are combined with
modern features to
create a luxurious home.

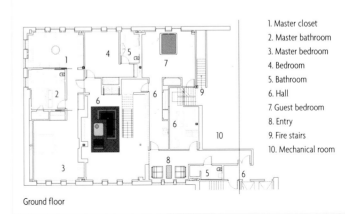

1. Master closet
2. Master bathroom
3. Master bedroom
4. Bedroom
5. Bathroom
6. Hall
7. Guest bedroom
8. Entry
9. Fire stairs
10. Mechanical room

Ground floor

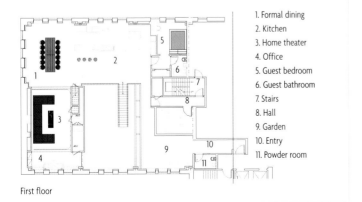

1. Formal dining
2. Kitchen
3. Home theater
4. Office
5. Guest bedroom
6. Guest bathroom
7. Stairs
8. Hall
9. Garden
10. Entry
11. Powder room

First floor

126

Transparent elements,
see-through curtains, and
careful lighting reflect
the architect's romantic,
minimalist approach.

House Turned Outside-In

Architect: Rooijakkers +
Tomesen Architecten
Location: Doetinchem,
The Netherlands
Date of construction: 2007
Photography: Luuk Kramer

This home is a contemporary alternative to the typical Dutch courtyard house, designed within the existing walls of a former dwelling. By swapping the outside and the inside, the home is completely redefined: The courtyard becomes the heart of the home as well as the axis for distribution of rooms.

Floor plan

1. Stairs
2. Hall
3. Kitchen
4. Scullery
5. Living room
6. Patio
7. Recessed balcony
8. Master bedroom
9. Master bathroom
10. Fitness room
11. Study
12. Guest bedroom
13. Guest bathroom
14. Shop
15. Home

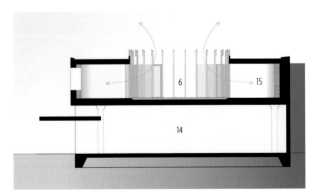

Section

127

A calm atmosphere reigns
in the main living area.
The use of natural
materials draws the eye
to the courtyard.

A deep bay window allows the inhabitant to step to the town beyond without actually leaving the house.

Cupboards built into the outside wall offer plenty of storage space without affecting the room's serene atmosphere.

130

The central courtyard floods
the home with natural light
and creates a protected, yet
open urban home.

131

The bedrooms and library are situated in the most protected places behind the solid facade.

The rooms that are far removed
from the courtyard and have no view
benefit from the use of impressionistic
lights and colors.

Courtyard House

This small simple house is located in Melbourne's inner city and its interior plan is driven by open spaces—some private, others open to the public realm. The plan divides the house into three zones: a study-library at the front, a living room-dining area in the center and bedrooms and other wet areas at the back of the house. The main living space faces the principal courtyard.

Architect: O'Connor + Houle
Architecture
Location: Melbourne, Australia
Date of construction: 2006
Photography: Trevor Mein

Floor plan

1. Driveway	6. Reading area	11. Bedroom	16. Pool
2. Garden	7. Living room	12. Bathroom	17. Patio
3. Entry	8. Dining room	13. Laundry room	18. Storage room
4. Gallery	9. Kitchen	14. Master bedroom	19. Garage
5. Study	10. WC	15. Master bathroom	

132

Floor-to-ceiling sliding doors open up the main living area to the outside, creating a continuum between interior and exterior.

133

A long horizontal window
in the wall (above) offers a
panorama of the street
though its translucence
ensures visual and
acoustic privacy.

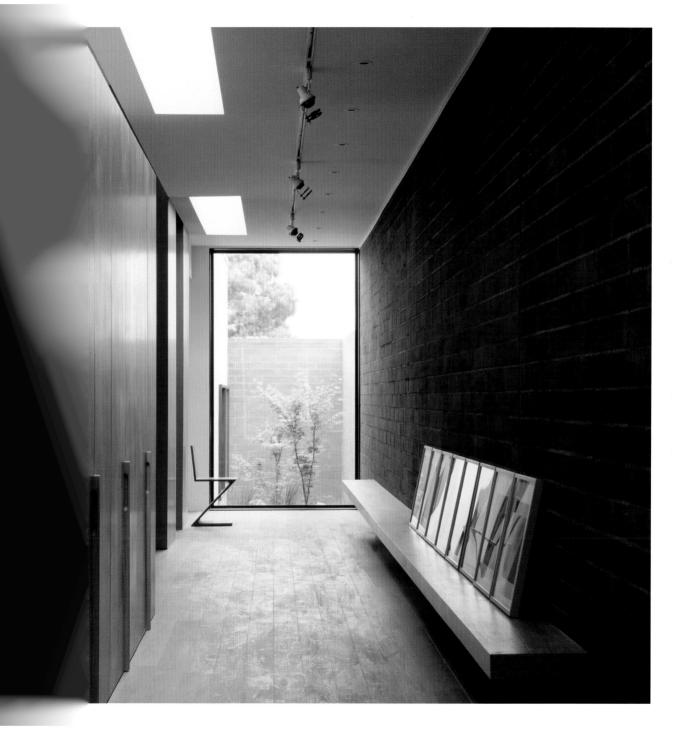

134

The arrangement of rooms
polarizes private and public
spaces: The day areas are
at the front, and night
areas are at the back
of the house.

Ng Residence

Architect: Toba + Paik
Location: New York, NY, U.S.A.
Date of construction: 2004
Photography: Mikiko Kukiyama

This 2,400-square-foot apartment is located in an apartment building that was originally designed as women's housing in Manhattan's West Village. The original exposed beams and the ceiling height posed difficulties in terms of creating a fluid two-story space. To reflect the client's exuberance and joie de vivre as well as meet his need for space to dance and entertain, the design needed to overcome existing conditions to keep the loft's open feel.

1. Mechanical room
2. Library
3. Office
4. Shower room
5. Bathroom
6. Sauna
7. Pantry
8. Hall
9. TV area
10. Kitchen
11. Living room
12. Dining room

Ground floor

1. Storage room
2. Closet
3. Master bedroom
4. Master bathroom
5. Hall

First floor

135

Each space is defined with
an architectural feature:
the fireplace in the living
area and the staircase
in the corridor, for example.

Allisma Residence

The architect and owner of this residence converted his former bedroom and an adjacent room in his father's home into a cross-programmed space that can serve multiple functions. To make the most of the tiny, 390-square-foot space, the original 8-inch ceiling on the upper level was torn down, the roof was restructured to make use of the full ceiling height, and six skylights were added to allow daylight to flood the interior. Additionally, the architect-owner came up with clever space-saving solutions.

Architect: **Tom Allisma**
Location: **Omaha, NE, U.S.A.**
Date of construction: **2004**
Photography: **Tom Kessler**

1. Entry
2. Bathroom
3. Stairs
4. Bedroom/Gallery/
   Gathering
5. Bedroom
6. Kitchen
7. Closet
8. Living room
9. Loft

Section   Ground floor   First floor

A platform created 8 feet above the floor holds a television, wine cooler, and stereo equipment. A closet on rollers also acts as a ladder and flip-up chair.

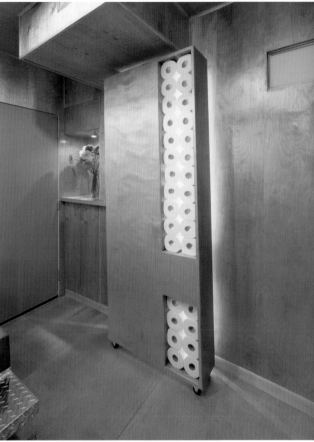

137

A cabinet on coasters
provides extra storage space
and doubles as a rolling
door to screen the restroom
on the lower level.

Bona Maggi

Architect: Lazzaro Raboni, Giuso
Della Giusta, Susanna Scarano
Location: Milan, Italy
Date of construction: 2002
Photography: Andrea
Martiradonna

Located in Isola, one of Milan's most traditional neighborhoods, this former workshop was turned into the home of a Milanese *signora* (lady). Though the characteristic windows let in plenty of light, the facing street promised little privacy. Thus, the windows were etched to make them translucent. This allows views of the sky, without permitting intrusions from outside. A mezzanine was created in the darkest part of the space for private areas.

138

The characteristic windows of this former workshop were etched to ensure privacy without forgoing the flood of natural light.

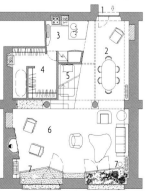

Ground floor

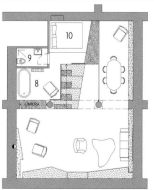

Mezzanine

1. Entry
2. Dining room
3. Kitchen
4. Closet
5. Guest space
6. Living room
7. Covered balcony
8. Bathroom
9. WC
10. Bedroom

139

A small alcove for guests was carved out of the space under the staircase leading to the exposed bathing area on the next level.

140

The kitchen and a closet
sit beneath the mezzanine
in the darker back
of the house.

Loft A3-3

This 2,099-square-foot loft—one of three in a former textile school—was designed for a family with one child. An extraordinary 5- by 52-foot structure was placed in the center of the space. This separates various functional areas on the second floor and connects spatial arrangements on the third floor. Thanks to openings and transparent elements in this volume, the clients can enjoy the length and width of the space.

Architect: NAT Architecten
Location: Eindhoven,
The Netherlands
Date of construction: 2005
Photography: Peter Cuypers

141

A long, stretched volume
in the center of the
space permits different
functions on either side
of the volume.

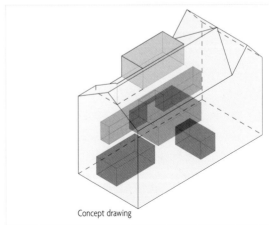

Concept drawing

1. Entry
2. WC
3. Closet
4. Elevator
5. Kitchen
6. Dining room
7. Chill-out area
8. TV area
9. Aquarium
10. Transparent fireplace
11. Loggia
12. Installations

13. Bridge
14. Balcony
15. Bedroom
16. Children's bedroom
17. Bathroom
18. Roof terrace

Second floor

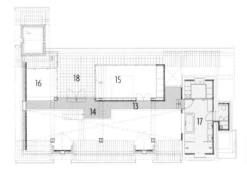

Third floor

142

A part of the second
floor is raised to create a
more intimate area,
a sort of platform from
which the third floor is
easily accessed.

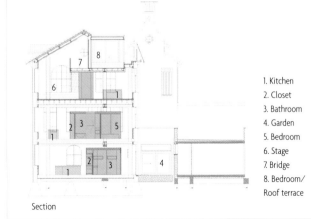

1. Kitchen
2. Closet
3. Bathroom
4. Garden
5. Bedroom
6. Stage
7. Bridge
8. Bedroom/
Roof terrace

Section

143

The bathroom has been
endowed with a sacred feel.
The design incorporates
existing elements and black
tiles on the walls.

Loft in Cuvio

Architect: Architectural Studio
Simone Micheli
Location: Cuvio, Italy
Date of construction: 2006
Photography: S.M.A.H.

This charming seventeenth-century residence near Varese with its rough-hewn structure, massive stone walls, old wooden beams, and openings with depressed arches has been converted into a spectacular modern home. A combination of voids, dynamic curves, volumetric features and unusual geometric elements distinguish the spirit of the house. These elements and others give this home on three levels enormous expressive power.

144

By taking out the
intermediate floor,
a cathedral ceiling could be
created for the living area
on the first floor.

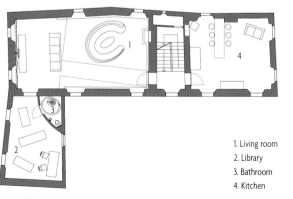

1. Living room
2. Library
3. Bathroom
4. Kitchen

Ground floor

145

The bridge with white plasterboard sides is a key architectural feature of the main living space and leads to a number of rooms on the upper level.

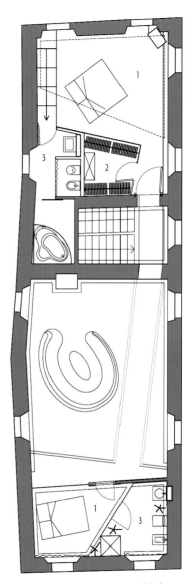

1. Bedroom
2. Closet
3. Bathroom

First floor

Storefront Loft

Step inside two large steel doors of an unforgiving block in New York's Alphabet City neighborhood to find a unique living space designed for an alternative couple and their collection of art and modern furniture. The only interesting features of this space were the 12-foot ceilings, steel columns, and thick wooden beams. The architects' intention was to create an abstract space with its own urban form. Each area is defined by architecture, though function is abstracted, hidden, and obscured.

Architect: Messana
O'Rorke Architects
Location: New York, NY, U.S.A.
Date of construction: 2005
Photography: Elizabeth Felicella

146

The kitchen blends into the space in the shape of a white lacquer and stainless steel orthogonal form. A wall of opaque plastic simulates sunshine opposite the entry.

1. Entry
2. Kitchen
3. Study
4. Living room
5. Bedroom
6. Bathroom
7. Closet

Floor plan

A high slot window in the large open space provides views of the sky to the south, while a 50-foot linear light fixture illuminates the gallery.

The function of the rooms
is abstracted, hidden, and
obscured: Each space are
identified by a sofa, a table,
or a bed.

Loft in Boulogne

Architect: Eric Chabeur
Location: Boulogne 92
(Paris), France
Date of construction: 2002
Photography: Stephen
Clément/Inside

A forty something couple with four children transformed two apartments in a 1930s suburban apartment building into an open-plan living space. The key materials chosen for the interior were concrete, steel, and wood. The combination of these materials make for a relaxed, modern, and flexible home, while the addition of thick steel ceiling supports give the place an industrial edge.

149

The imposing concrete
staircase is the centerpiece
of this suburban home and
acts as a natural divider.

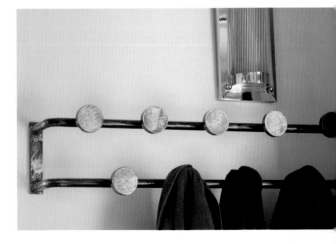

150

The combination of antiques
and a concrete kitchen
island produces an
unusual living space.
All five bedrooms are
on the top floor.